A GUIDED HOLOCAUST REMEMBRANCE

MOMENT OF WITNESS

Deborah Fripp and Violet Neff-Helms

BEHRMAN HOUSE
www.behrmanhouse.com

This is for every community that has ever felt the pain of violence and hate.

The publisher gratefully acknowledges these editorial consultants for their contributions to *Light from the Darkness*, from which this book is adapted: Ellen Rank, educator; Rabbi Perry Rank; Rabbi Jonah Rank; Lynne Ravas, Holocaust educator; Rabbi Danny Zemel; Diane Zimmerman, educator.

Copyright © 2025 Deborah Fripp and Violet Neff-Helms
All rights reserved. No part of this publication may be translated, reproduced, stored in a retrieval system or transmitted, in any form or by any means, electronic, mechanical, photocopying, recording or otherwise, for any purpose, without express written permission from the publishers.

Behrman House, Inc.
Millburn, New Jersey
www.behrmanhouse.com

ISBN 978-1-68115-157-1

Library of Congress Control Number: 2024938232

Edited by Aviva Lucas Gutnick
Cover design by Cassie Gonzales
Book design by Zatar Creative and Elynn Cohen

Printed in China

9 8 7 6 5 4 3 2 1

CONTENTS

SYMBOLS iv
INTRODUCTION 1
LIGHT AND DARKNESS 2
BEGINNINGS 4
TROUBLES 6
HIDING 8
TERROR 10
HELP 14
STRENGTH 16
LIFE 18
MEMORY 20
AWAKENING 22
COMMUNITY 24
HOPE 26
RESOLVE 28
STORIES 32
COMMUNITIES 36
LEADER'S GUIDE 38
DISCUSSION QUESTIONS 40
ACKNOWLEDGMENTS 42
ABOUT THE AUTHORS 42
SOURCES, CREDITS 43
STILL STANDS 44

SYMBOLS

HERE ARE THE SYMBOLS WE WILL ENCOUNTER AND USE TODAY:

Mismatched candlesticks: in recognition of the resilience of our ancestors

Fruit with pits: for inner strength and an unbreakable core

Wine or juice: in celebration of life

Tea candles: in memory of the murdered millions

Bread: in celebration of community

Paper/pen: for hope and action

Bread crusts: for sharing in the starving times

INTRODUCTION

Today we journey through one of the darkest chapters in history.

We know that the Holocaust was a campaign by Germany to exterminate the Jewish people. But the Holocaust is not only a Jewish story, although it is a story about Jews. The Holocaust is not only a German story, although it is a story about Germans. The Holocaust is a human story. It is our collective story—one of both heroes and villains, of victims and saviors. It is a story about the potential both for cruelty and for kindness, in every community, in every person.

We are here for a moment of witness. Today we remember the people who experienced the Holocaust firsthand: the victims and the bystanders, the survivors and the rescuers—and yes, even the perpetrators. We take inspiration from the resilience and strength of the victims and those who stood up against hatred and cruelty.

We are collectively the descendants of the Holocaust. We are the descendants of the victims and of the perpetrators, of those who stood by and of those who stood up, of those who were uninvolved and of those who were unaware. We each have a relationship to the story. In this moment, we raise our own voices—individually and collectively—and see our own lives in this mirror. We learn that by our vigilance and by our actions, we can help prevent our communities from walking toward hatred and violence.

At this guided remembrance, we gather across different faiths and backgrounds to remember. We use objects that unite us: candles, wine, bread, and fruit. In addition to worship, these items have ordinary uses. We invoke that ordinariness today. Today, they are neither the Sabbath candles nor the seder wine, neither the sacrifice of the Mass nor part of Communion. Today, they are ordinary objects that provide a tangible connection to our history.

We will draw ourselves into the story of the Holocaust in a personal way. We will also ask questions to connect our own experiences and the experiences of our communities to the deeply troubling issues raised by this history.

LIGHT AND DARKNESS

The world had been broken. The shards exposed a pattern of pain and devastation.

The Holocaust was not the first genocide, and sadly it was not the last. But the Holocaust awoke the world. The documentation—cold, clinical, and often made by the perpetrators themselves—left us with an undeniable record. An archive of atrocity.

This story teaches us to gather every precious remnant of our broken world and piece them back together. We are somehow whole and broken at the same time.

In recollecting the Holocaust, together we discover glimmers of holiness through these cracks, for it is in them that we see the paths to building a better tomorrow.

"Blessed is the match consumed in kindling flame. Blessed is the flame that burns in the secret fastness of the heart."
(Hannah Senesh, Holocaust refugee, left safety of Palestine to fight in Hungary against the Nazis)

Rose and Barbed Wire,
Shmuel Leitner

We resolve to follow the strength and courage of those who stood fast for righteousness. Even when enveloped by evil, we will hold on to our faith in humanity.

RECITE:

We will emerge strengthened in our resolve to work for a better future.

CANDLE LIGHTING

Candles are at once a symbol of Jewish holy days and a beacon to guide us through the darkness. These mismatched candlesticks remind us that even when we do not have all that we need, we can be a light in the darkness. We take inspiration from those who made do with what they had. We take strength from those who found the strength to stand when standing seemed impossible.

LIGHT THE CANDLES AND RECITE:

We light these candles for the light that shines in the hearts of all who fight against evil, for a single candle can both defy and define the darkness.

PAUSE FOR A MOMENT OF SILENCE.

BEGINNINGS

The story of genocide begins with people. Each individual has a story, a life that began before the darkness fell.

No matter who our ancestors were, we step into these stories as if they were our own.

We remember the life before:

> Not so long ago, many of us lived in the lands of Europe and North Africa. We lived together, side by side, with Christians, Muslims, and others, as neighbors and as friends.
>
> We were Jews of many different sorts. We were religious and secular. We lived in cities and in small towns. We lived in many countries across the world. We spoke many different languages. We were doctors and dressmakers, printers and poets, scientists and shopkeepers, weavers and welders.

"We were a warm family whose life followed a quiet, carefree routine. Our roots reached back generation upon generation, living there amidst friends, neighbors, and acquaintances. With this loving background, the years flowed peacefully."

(Miriam Yahav, Holocaust survivor, Poland)

View of Ostende with Boat, 1935, Felix Nussbaum, gouache on paper

As a community, we acknowledge our collective refusal to see:

> An ancient hatred, undisguised, was emerging from the shadows. While Jews faced violence and discrimination in many places, we held to our belief that it was not the case in our homes or among our neighbors. We believed we had grown beyond such ignorance. We did not recognize the approaching danger.

FOR A SWEET, FLAVORFUL LIFE

We, the descendants of all these peoples, drink together, as friends and neighbors do, in memory of the sweet, flavorful life before the darkness fell.

RAISE THE WINE/JUICE GLASSES AND RECITE:
L'chaim! To life!

DRINK THE WINE OR JUICE.

Moment of Witness
Have you witnessed prejudice? When did you realize this? What did you do?

TROUBLES

The path to genocide is often neither swift nor straight. Time after time, the path to genocide has been a slow-burning fuse of degrading language and subtle discrimination. When we ignore the slowly rising shadows of hatred, those shadows can engulf us.

We are all born with a desire to love, not a desire to hate. Without a watchful eye, we can slide into ancient prejudices.

We remember (and speak as the Jews of Germany might have):

> Hatred spread across Germany like poison in water.

> The Germans afflicted us with cruel laws and humiliations. They did not care who we were or what we did. They did not care whether we were religious or secular, from the city or from the country, civilian or soldier, only that we were Jews.

Trouble does not begin with fanfare, but as storm clouds building in the distance.

> "Every day they keep issuing new laws against Jews. Today for example, they took all our appliances away from us: the sewing machine, the radio, the telephone, the vacuum cleaner, the electric fryer, my camera, and my bicycle. . . . Agi said we should be happy they're taking things and not people." (**Eva Heyman,** Holocaust victim, Romania)

We remember:

> Many of us fled. Many more tried to flee but found there was no place to go. Some who thought we had found safe haven were sent back into danger.

> The Germans crowded us into small ghettos cut off from the outside world. There was never enough food. Death was a daily visitor.

Rear Entrance, Terezin Ghetto, 1941-1944,
Bedřich Fritta, India ink and wash on paper

In these overcrowded ghettos, we lamented, "I feel as if I am in a box. There is no air to breathe. Wherever you go, you encounter a gate that hems you in. I feel as if I have been robbed, my freedom is being robbed from me, my home, and the familiar streets I love so much. I have been cut off from all that is dear and precious to me."

(**Yitzkhok Rudashevski**, Holocaust victim, Lithuania)

Many Jews fought for their countries in World War I. But their service did not protect them. In Germany in the 1930s, Jews were banned from riding the trains and forbidden to drive. They could shop only during a few short hours and only from Jewish-owned stores. They could not even sit in their own gardens in the evenings. Their children were forbidden from attending school.

THE TEARS OF THE GHETTO

TAKE A BIT OF BREAD CRUST.

For many of us, breaking bread together is a symbol of fellowship. This crust of bread reminds us that when we are starving, we eat whatever we can find. But even in dark times, we share the scraps.

RECITE:

For ashes I ate like bread, and my drinks I mixed with weeping.
(**Psalm 102:10**)

EAT THE BREAD CRUST.

Moment of Witness

What stories of hate and persecution have touched you? How did you respond?

HIDING

Hate is unashamed. It can present itself in its full, raw fury. Yet it can also present itself in flowery words and with broad smiles. It can cloak itself in flags and sings of better days gone by. While it distracts our attention with petty squabbles, its poison saps the vigor of society.

As a community we acknowledge:

> When our neighbors began to disappear from our communities, it was not done in the dark. We knew that terrible things were happening to them. Most of us chose silence, to look away, and to ignore the hate.

> We waited. We waited to see when the cruelty would end. We waited for the hate to pass. We waited too long.

When we hide from the truth of what we are witnessing, we allow hatred to grow and violence to spread.

We remember both the hope and the fear:

> Holding on to the hope that we might one day be reunited, we sent our children into hiding. A few were sent to safety beyond the German borders. Others found hiding places with friends, neighbors, and strangers. As we sent our young children away, alone, our grief for the separation overlaid our prayers for their survival.

> "As Mommy and Omi waved to me, I chose to hide my tears, and I smiled. I wanted to give them strength." (**Ruth Westheimer**, survivor, Germany)

Moment of Witness
Can you think of a time when you were silent while others were mistreated? Why do you think people hide from the truth of what they're witnessing?

FAITH IN THE FUTURE

We, the descendants of both bystanders and victims, remember how families separated in hope of survival. We weep for them. Where did they find such hope?

READ TOGETHER:

Hope and faith may seem frail comfort, but they are steel girders that give us the strength to stand.

TAKE A SLIP OF PAPER. WRITE ON IT A HOPE FOR THE FUTURE—A PERSONAL HOPE OR A HOPE FOR YOUR COMMUNITY.

These notes represent our hopes for ourselves and our children. They represent our faith in the future.

Let these hopes be a sweetness that lies beneath the bitterness.

As we all did in the time of trouble, we now conceal our hope in a secret place to keep it safe. May we find it again at the end of our journey.

FOLD THE SLIP OF PAPER. HIDE IT IN A SAFE PLACE FROM WHERE IT CAN EASILY BE RETRIEVED.

"For two years, we lived with them. For two years, I did not leave the building. For two years, I did not walk around the apartment. For two years, I did not go near a window—I would always crawl underneath."

(Hannah Gofrit, Holocaust survivor, Poland)

TERROR

Words fail as we speak of the darkest times.

We remember:

A mixed multitude were caught in the Nazis' web of death: Jews, Romani, gay people, people with disabilities, voices of resistance. Many of us died at the Nazis' hands. A special viciousness was aimed at the Jews and the Romani, two cultures the Germans were determined to eradicate.

We remember:

The Germans murdered us Jews in staggering numbers. In many places, bystanders became willing participants in the violence. We were murdered without mercy: mothers and fathers, children and grandparents. We were murdered simply for being Jews.

We remember:

For generations, we Romani have wandered free throughout Europe, yet were distrusted and shunned. Strong families helped us endure until the terror of the Devouring. The Germans murdered us alongside the Jews, simply for being who we are. Mass graves filled the forests of Europe.

We remember:

The Germans tore us from our homes, forcing us into slave labor camps and into death chambers. Those who could not work were murdered. Those who could work were kept as slaves until they too succumbed to starvation and illness.

"In our blind ignorance, we thought that deportation was a better solution. Fools that we were, we thought that the ghetto was the ultimate in abysmal blackness. We did not know that from here on, we would be severed and cut off from everything that was familiar and dear to us. We did not know that from that train ride on, we would be robbed of our whole world." (**Sara Selver**, Holocaust survivor, Poland)

THE LOST COMMUNITIES

LIGHT THE TEA CANDLES.

In their mission to obliterate civilizations, the Germans wiped out whole communities – not only their present but also their history and their future. The sudden silence, this multigenerational emptiness, takes our breath away.

These communities had existed since the time when Jews were enslaved by the Romans. They were refugees from the Inquisition. They endured the Crusades and survived the pogroms. But they are no more.

READ RESPONSIVELY.

A millennium of wisdom erased. And a whole generation emptied of artists and writers, of scholars and teachers. An entire library of poems unwritten, music unimagined, knowledge unexplored.

We mourn centers of learning: Vilna, Vienna, Prague

Two thousand years of civilization wiped away. And a whole generation silenced of love and laughter, of charity and celebration. An entire society of families unborn, stories untold, synagogues unbuilt.

We mourn centers of life: Sarajevo, Salonika, Chelm, Warsaw

A legacy of industry and craft extinguished. A whole generation bereft of artisans and builders, of experts and leaders. An entire economy of things unmade, science undiscovered, medicine unpracticed.

We mourn centers of progress: Kiev, Kielce, Frankfurt

There are so many more: thousands of communities, millions of people. All silenced.

Let these lights shine as a symbol of life and love remembered. May they illuminate our memory and guide our future.

PAUSE FOR A MOMENT OF SILENCE

TERROR (CONTINUED)

Winter, 1944, Zinovii Tolkatchev
charcoal and crayon on paper

The Nazis targeted a number of non-Jewish groups, including gay men, people with mental disabilities, political dissidents, and the Romani ethnic group, European nomads derogatorily known as gypsies. The Romani call the Holocaust the *Porajmos*, which means "the Devouring." Almost 50 percent of European Romani were murdered in the *Porajmos*. The Romani culture survived, and they remain the largest ethnic minority in Europe. More about the Romani can be found on page 36. The stories of some European Jewish communities can be found on page 32.

FROM DARKNESS INTO LIGHT

We pause in terror before the human deed
The cloud of annihilation,
the concentration of death
The cruelly casual way of each to each.
But in the stillness of this hour,
We find our way from darkness into light.

(Chaim Stern)

Moment of Witness
Wide-scale violence has brutalized many communities around the world. Has such violence come close to you or your community? In whose voice do you remember these stories?

HELP

How do we stay hopeful when people are capable of such great evil?

Some good people recognized the evil for what it was. A few were willing to risk their lives to help. They hid friends, neighbors, and strangers from the eyes of those bent on harm. In almost every survivor's story, there is a story of someone who helped.

These people are our ancestors too.

We know:

> Rescuers lived in every country in Europe. We came from every walk of life. Some saved hundreds. Some saved one. We did all we could to save as many as we could, regretting only that we could not do more.

> Having been their nanny for thirteen years, twenty-six-year-old Erzsebet Fajo swore she would protect the Abonyi family. As the bombs fell on Budapest and the fascist militias searched the streets for Jews, Erzsebet risked her life daily to find a safe place for each family member to hide. "She saved us day by day." (**Zsuzsanna Abonyi Ozsváth,** Holocaust survivor, Hungary)

> Sister Gertruda Marciniak ran an orphanage and a home for girls suffering from tuberculosis in Poland. Exploiting the German's fear of contagious diseases, she used the home as a cover to hide Jewish children. Once, when Nazis came to search the home, she hid little Dan Landsberg under her habit, standing motionless until the Nazis left. "Once a child has come to me, their fate will be my fate too." (**Sister Gertruda Stanislawa Marciniak,** Holocaust rescuer, Poland)

> In some places, whole communities stood together to protect Jews. For the mostly Muslim population of Albania, helping Jews was a matter of national honor. When the Germans invaded Albania, Nuro Hoxha, a teacher and a religious Muslim, hid four Jewish families in underground bunkers in his house. "Now we are one family," he told them. "My sons and I will defend you against peril at the cost of our lives." (**Nuro Hoxha,** Holocaust rescuer, Albania)

INSPIRATION

We, the descendants of bystanders, rescuers, and survivors honor the helpers so that we may gain wisdom from them. We must always strive for the courage to help those in need.

STAND AND TAKE THE HAND OF ANOTHER PARTICIPANT OR REACH YOUR ARMS TOWARD EACH OTHER.

RECITE:

We reach for each other in fellowship and peace, pulling each other to safety.

Each person's decision to help was difficult. The risks were many. Would we have made such a decision? We cannot know. We cannot judge.

In gratitude and hope, we honor the helpers. We draw inspiration from them, and vow never to be indifferent to the plight of others.

Strength comes to those who pursue justice.

RELEASE HANDS AND BE SEATED.

Liberation, Shmuel Leitner

"I do not know what a Jew is; we only know what human beings are."

(**Pastor André Trocmé**, Holocaust rescuer, France)

Moment of Witness
How do we recognize when others need help? What could we be listening for?

STRENGTH

An army arrayed to eliminate the future, but they could not erase the memory of an entire culture. Bodies could be destroyed but the Jewish spirit could not be defeated.

We remember:

> Despite our enemies' eagerness to strip us of our Judaism and our humanity, we continued to educate our children, to celebrate our holidays, to love and help each other.

> Although prayer was forbidden, we prayed in secret communities and within the secret places in our hearts. "Our faith was the one thing they could not take from us." **(Rivka Wagner,** Holocaust survivor, Poland)

> Hidden between the bunks, we whispered the familiar words of the Sabbath prayers and found tranquility. "I discovered for the first time in my life the real power and value of prayer and faith in God. I could feel my words shattering the iron gates and the high-powered fences, going past the hundreds of guards, dugouts, and watchtowers, out into the open, reaching towards heaven. Here, I knew, was a way of escape, a source of strength, and a means of survival of which no power on earth could deprive me." **(Simcha Unsdorfer,** Holocaust survivor, Czechoslovakia)

Camp Synagogue in Saint Cyprien, 1941, Felix Nussbaum, oil on plywood

Moment of Witness
What does "strength" mean to you?

In the ghetto, a young boy defied the bitterness.

FROM TOMORROW ON

>From tomorrow on, I shall be sad—
From tomorrow on.
Today I will be happy.

What's the use of sadness—tell me that?
Because the evil winds begin to blow?
Why should I grieve for tomorrow—
today?

No, today I will be glad.

And every day, no matter how bitter it be,
I will say:
From tomorrow on, I shall be sad—
Not today.

(**Motele**, a child in the ghetto, excerpted)

THE UNBREAKABLE CORE

We honor the strength of those who held onto their faith in humanity. These fruits, with their unbreakable inner core, represent our ancestors' inner strength. They are a tangible token of the power to resist.

We eat these fruits so that we may gain courage to find our own inner strength in difficult times.

HOLD UP A FRUIT WITH A PIT AND RECITE TOGETHER:

If one has courage, nothing can dim the light that shines from within.
   (Maya Angelou)

EAT THE FRUIT.

LIFE

Liberation did come. As the armies of the world moved toward vanquishing this evil, they discovered a hell that left them stunned.

We remember:

> As we survivors emerged from that hell, we asked: How do we move forward when we have lost so much?

> We walk with a hole in our hearts and weight in our footsteps, but we walk forward. We are reduced, but we refuse to remain broken.

> While the world counted their dead, we counted our living. Those who lived gave us the strength to love again.

> We did not know what would come next. We only knew we could not go back to the life we once lived.

As a community we acknowledge:

> As we watched our neighbors struggle to regain their footing, we found our own footing not quite so steady. For we remembered what we had been taught: "Truly I tell you, whatever you did for one of the least of these brothers and sisters of mine, you did for me." **(Matthew 25:40)**

> We wished we had done more.

> We know that we must reach out to all souls in need.

RECITE:

Only by loving our neighbors with all our hearts can we heal the terrible hurt that has been done to the world.

One Spring, 1941, Karl Robert Bodek and Kurt Conard Löw
watercolor, India ink and pencil on paper

Moment of Witness
What does it mean to love our neighbors with all our hearts? What gets in the way?

THEIR TEARS IN OUR HANDS

Let us strive to be that light in the world. As it is written, "Love the whole world as a mother loves her only child." (paraphrased from the Buddhist **Karaniya Metta Sutta**)

LIFT YOUR HANDS AND TURN THE PALMS FACING UP. RECITE:

We take their sorrow into our hands, to cleanse, to heal, to protect. We reveal our palms to express our hope, for hands are an extension of the heart.

Words are not enough. It takes our hands to build.

MEMORY

Our hope for the future is tempered by our tears for the past. We drown in the enormity of our emptiness, lost in the ocean of the absence of those lost. Most of what remains is memory. We cling to this memory as we acknowledge that they lived.

RECITE:

As long as we remember them, they are with us.

The survivors entreat us, "I ask you not to forget the dead. I ask you to build a memorial in our names, a monument reaching up to the heavens, that the entire world might see. Not a monument of marble or stone, but one of good deeds. I believe with full and perfect faith that only such a monument can promise a better future. Only thus can we be sure that the evil that overturned the world and turned our lives into hell will never return."
(adapted from **Donia Rosen**, Holocaust survivor, Ukraine)

THE LOST

Let us remember them as they lived. As we contemplate their pictures, we mourn the stories cut short, the prayers unanswered and dreams lost. We speak their names, so they will not be forgotten.

Some people in these photos are not named, reminding us that although some stories are lost, we still acknowledge the people who lived them. For these, we simply say, "Unknown." Let these few represent for us the many.

READ THE NAMES.

Gisi Fleischmann Rudi Salmang Unknown Zipporah Picker Shraga Picker

Settela Steinbach Yehiel Mintzberg Henryk Szwarc Izabel Marton Zoli Marton

Taleskoten, 1944, Zinovii Tolkatchev
gouache, charcoal and crayon on paper

Moment of Witness
What responsibility do we have to the victims of the Holocaust and other genocides?

OPTIONAL: **ASK FOR THE NAMES OF ADDITIONAL VICTIMS OF THE HOLOCAUST OR OTHER HATE CRIMES**

Let us pause for a moment of silent reflection.

TAKE A MOMENT OF SILENCE.

We remember not only the uncountable Jewish and Romani dead, but also the many who were murdered alongside them: gay people, people with disabilities, and voices of resistance, all murdered in the great silencing of diversity, speech, and opposition.

THEY ARE GONE

They are gone.
They cannot tell their stories any longer.
But we can.
We can hold open the window, this fragile window,
We can give their stories wings.
Let us give their stories a voice, so they can fly into others' ears, into others' hearts.

RECITE:

Only we can tell their stories now.
Only we.
(Jennifer Rudick Zunikoff)

PAUSE FOR A MOMENT OF SILENCE

AWAKENING

In the aftermath of this horror, we awaken to a world where human beings have done unfathomable evil to each other. What do we do now?

Bereft, we weep: How do we mourn so many lost, so many murdered?

We recall each story, each name, each life. We remember how they were caught up, one by one, in the web of hate. We remember their strength, how they held on to love and life and hope, even in the harshest times. Their stories teach us that the thread of life is strong. As survivors say, "Grandchildren are the best revenge."

Overwhelmed, we whisper: I do not want to hear any more.

We draw inward to comfort one another. We remember that "even as we grieve, we grow; even as we hurt, we hope; even as we tire, we try." (Adapted from **Amanda Gorman**)

We know that ignoring evil only allows it to grow. Despite our unease, we choose not to be blind. We choose awareness because we recognize that "evil does not need our help, just our indifference." (Adapted from **Hanns Loewenbach**, Holocaust refugee, Germany to America)

Angered, we cry out: How could this happen? Where was the world?

We remember not only the cruelty of those bent on harm but also the compassion of those few determined to help. We resolve to turn our anger into a passionate drive to make the world a better place for everyone.

Awakened, we inquire: How does such hatred grow? How can we stop it?

Hatred grows when we ignore it, when we allow hateful behavior to go unchallenged. We will not let evil hide in the shadows. We resolve to shine a spotlight on hate and make it clear that such behavior is not acceptable. We will be vocal torchbearers of love.

> "Learn from yesterday, live for today, hope for tomorrow. The important thing is not to stop questioning."
> (**Albert Einstein**, Holocaust refugee, Germany to America)

View of Buchenwald, a Few Days After Liberation, 1945, Jakob Zim, watercolor on paper

AN AFFIRMATION FOR THE FUTURE

READ RESPONSIVELY:

I pray for courage, and for strength.
When I remember the evils in the past,
The innocent people tortured and murdered,
I am almost afraid to make myself remember.
But I am even more afraid to forget.

> I ask for wisdom, that I might mourn,
> And not be consumed by hatred.
> That I might remember,
> And yet not lose hope.

I must face evil—
And, so doing, reaffirm my faith in future good.
I cannot erase yesterday's pains,
But I can vow that they will not have suffered in vain.

> And so I pray:
> For those who were given death, I choose life
> For me and for generations yet to come.

For those who found courage to stand against evil—
Often at the cost of their lives—
I vow to carry on their struggle.

> I must teach myself, and others
> to learn from hatred that people must love,
> to learn from evil to live for good.

(Anonymous)

Moment of Witness
What "evils in the past" linger in your mind? How can you make that memory a tool with which to work for good?

COMMUNITY

The Nazis stoked divisions by setting groups against one another. Many communities drank this poison and were devoured. A few resisted. Communities that stood together saved thousands of lives. The people of Denmark, Sweden, Albania, Bulgaria, Finland, and Le Chambon in France protected their Jewish neighbors.

Even today, we continue to fight evil as it sows division among us. We seek healing by knitting our community together. We repair the world by weaving connections to one another.

Together, we celebrate our loves and our losses, our strength and our caring.

RECITE:

Working together, we can change the world.

HOLD UP THE BREAD

We share bread as a symbol of our shared community. From the abundance of our brightest lives to the sharing of scraps in the darkest times, communities rise with the sharing of bread. Jewish tradition understood this: "Let all who are hungry come and eat. Let all who are needy, come and celebrate with us." **(Passover Haggadah)** Let us take up that call, to share our friendship with all who are in need.

Moment of Witness

What is the pillar that enables your community to survive and thrive in difficult times?

"The offer of sharing bread was the first human gesture that occurred among us."

(Primo Levi, Holocaust survivor, Italy, recounting how in 1945 the Nazis left him alone with a group of other men in Auschwitz because they were too ill to march.)

RECITE TOGETHER:

We give thanks for our survival, acknowledging that we are no more deserving than those who did not survive.

We celebrate the Jewish community that continues to thrive and the community we have created between us today.

We bless the source of life that brings forth bread from the earth.
(The Book of Blessings)

EAT THE BREAD.

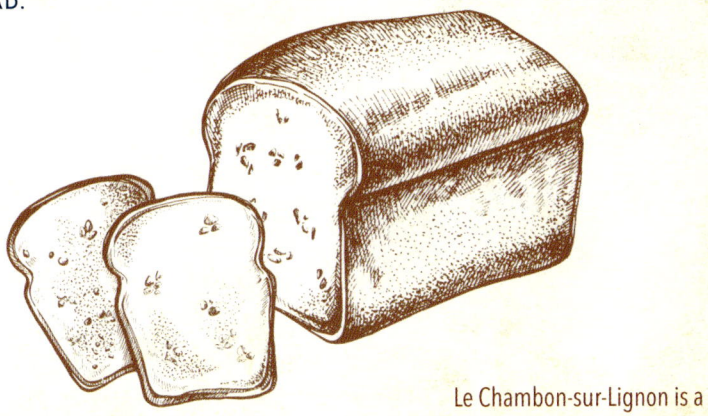

Le Chambon-sur-Lignon is a small village in south-central France. Between 1940 and 1944, Le Chambon and other nearby villages provided refuge for more than 5,000 people fleeing the Nazis.

HOPE

~~~~~~~~~~~~~~~~~~~~~~~~~~~~~~~~~~

We can all learn lessons from the Holocaust—from the victims, from the bystanders, from the rescuers, and even from the perpetrators.

We recognize the children of the perpetrators:

> Nothing we do can atone for what our parents did. We cannot change this past. It haunts us. It stains our lives. But we must not forget our inheritance of shame.

> We do not celebrate our parents' deeds. We pour over the broken shards of a world they shattered. We hold that legacy as a beacon, a lighthouse to warn of the perils of unchecked xenophobia and prejudice. For tragically, pieces of this story have been repeated all too often.

RECITE:

Despite our earnest efforts, people are still persecuted for who they are. Anger and hatred, nurtured by prejudice, continue to take root in our communities.

We, each one of us a descendant of the Holocaust, proclaim:

> *There is still hope. We each can make a difference.*

FIND THE HIDDEN SLIP OF PAPER WHERE YOU WROTE YOUR HOPE. BRING IT BACK OUT. READ IT TO YOURSELF.

These notes represent our hopes for ourselves and our children. When we stand with hope, we brace ourselves with determination.

But hope is not enough. We seek to turn that hope into a leap of action, and bring us into the light.

ON THE BACK OF THE PAPER, WRITE ONE STEP YOU CAN TAKE TO MOVE THAT HOPE INTO A REALITY.

OPTIONAL: SHARE ONE OR BOTH SIDES OF YOUR NOTE WITH A PARTNER OR THE GROUP.

WORDS OF PEACE

We cannot change our past, but we can work to build a future rooted in peace and justice.

We hope for peace and justice in our world. And we remember that peace and justice are not gifts from God. They are our gifts to each other. (adapted from **Elie Wiesel,** Holocaust survivor, Hungary)

Across this world, we are many different people. We speak many different languages. Peace is a gift we can give in every language.

READ WORDS OF PEACE ALOUD:

Asisti	KURDISH	هاسیتی	*Pache*	ITALIAN	Pace
Bizaanizi	OJIBWE	**Bizaanizi**	*Amaidhi*	TAMIL	அமைதி
Eirini	GREEK	Ειρήνη	*Pyonghwa*	KOREAN	평화
Freeden	GERMAN	Frieden	*Salám*	ARABIC	سلام
Frithur	ICELANDIC	Friður	*Samaya*	SINHALESE	සාමය
Heiwa	JAPANESE	平和	*Santiphap*	KHMER	សន្តិភាព
Meero	ROMANI	**Miro**	*Shaanti*	HINDI	शांति
Mir	RUSSIAN	Мир	*Shalom*	HEBREW	שלום

Moment of Witness
Do the descendants of the perpetrators have a place in the narrative? Do their voices matter? Why or why not?

RESOLVE

Through the windows of our broken history, we have seen bits of ourselves in all of these stories: in the victims and in the bystanders, in the perpetrators, and in the rescuers. As we recall the Holocaust, we resolve to follow the strength and courage of those who stood fast for righteousness.

We resolve to learn so that no people shall ever suffer such a fate again.

We say: Never Again.

NEVER AGAIN

READ RESPONSIVELY:

Never again shall we ignore the gathering shadows of hate.

Never again.

Never again shall we stay silent at the preaching of malice.

Never again..

Never again shall we excuse those who hate.

Never again.

RECITE TOGETHER:

"As long as poverty, injustice, and gross inequality persist in our world, none of us can truly rest." **(Nelson Mandela)**

READ RESPONSIVELY:

Never again shall we stand and watch while people are mistreated.

Never again.

Never again shall we allow groups of people to be separated and made unequal.

Never again.

Never again shall we watch a community plant the seeds of hate and do nothing.

Never again.

To the Man who Restored my Belief in Humanity, 1945, Yehuda Bacon, gouache, black chalk and pencil on paper

RECITE TOGETHER:

"If your eyes be turned toward justice, choose for your neighbor that which you choose for yourself."(**Bahá'u'lláh**)

READ RESPONSIVELY:

Never again shall we think we are helpless to stop the coming of evil.

Never again.

Never again shall we forget our own strength.

Never again.

Never again shall we allow hatred to go unanswered.

Never again.

RECITE TOGETHER:

"I raise up my voice not so I can shout but so that those without a voice can be heard." (**Malala Yousafzai**)

RESOLVE (CONTINUED)

TO WORK FOR JUSTICE

Let us raise our voices for those who cannot.
As it is written,
"Justice, justice you shall pursue"

RECITE TOGETHER:

Never again will we turn our faces from the cry for help.

The need is here, the need is now.

Justice, justice we shall pursue.

"Do not be dismayed by the brokenness of the world. All things break. And all things can be mended. Not with time, as they say, but with intention. So go. Love intentionally, extravagantly, unconditionally. The broken world waits in darkness for the light that is you." (L.R. Knost)

Moment of Witness

Where do you see the greatest need for justice right now? What steps can you take to pursue that end?

A DAY WILL COME

a day will come
when the softest sounds
will be enough

when one lingering note

a delicate dance
between two hands

a leaf spinning in
the breeze

when one ringing bell

when one whispered poem
will be enough

to awaken each person
from that which is concealed

to bless this holy human
with wisdom that bursts

from the sacred well of justice

from the sweet, hearty, bubbling
subterranean spring that nourishes
the Tree of Life

(Jennifer Rudick Zunikoff)

STORIES

STORIES OF THE HOLOCAUST VICTIMS, SURVIVORS, FIGHTERS, AND RESCUERS WHOSE WORDS AND ARTWORK APPEAR IN THIS BOOK:

Robert Antelme was part of a resistance group in France led by François Mitterand. He was deported to Buchenwald in 1944. On liberation, Mitterand pulled the living Antelme from a pile of dead bodies.

Yehuda Bacon was born in 1929 in Czechoslovakia. In 1942, he was sent to Terezin and then to Auschwitz. His sketches of the crematoria and gas chambers served as testimony at the Eichmann trial. He immigrated to Israel, where he joined the faculty of the Bezalel Academy of Art.

Karl Robert Bodek and **Kurt Conrad Löw** often collaborated on their artwork. Together, they prepared stage settings for the cabaret at the Gurs internment camp in France. Bodek was transported to Drancy and Auschwitz, where he was murdered. Löw was released and made his way to Geneva. He returned to Vienna, his birthplace, in 1952, where he lived until his death in 1980.

Albert Einstein was a professor at the Prussian Academy of Sciences in Berlin, already a Nobel Prize–winning physicist, in 1933. He was visiting the United States when Hitler came to power. He opted not to return to Germany, and became an American citizen in 1940.

Erzsebet Fajo was thirteen years old when she came to work for the Abonyi family in 1931. In 1944, when the family was in danger, she risked her life to save them. After the war, the Abonyis adopted her and paid for her education. She was recognized by Yad Vashem as "Righteous Among the Nations" in 1986.

Bedřich Fritta was a graphic designer and cartoonist in Prague. As director of the painting section of the Technical Department at the Terezin Ghetto, he was forced to provide propaganda material for the Germans. In secret, Fritta and his colleagues smuggled out paintings depicting the horrors of ghetto life. After these were discovered, Fritta was sent to Auschwitz, where he died.

Hannah Gofrit was born in 1935 in Biała Rawska, Poland. She spent the war hiding with her mother in the Warsaw home of non-Jewish friends. In 1949, she moved to Israel, where she became the chief nurse in Tel Aviv's Public Health Division.

Eva Heyman turned thirteen in 1944. Three days later she was deported to Auschwitz and eventually murdered. Her mother, Agi, survived the war but committed suicide in 1949.

Nuro Hoxha was a respected teacher in Tërbaç, Albania. For fourteen months, he hid four families in the storeroom of his cellar. Twice he risked his life to intervene with Albanian fascists to get members of the Jewish families out of prison.

Dan Landsberg was one of the children rescued by Sister Gertruda Marciniak. Sister Gertruda placed him with a Polish family for most of the war. Dan moved to Israel in 1965 and built a large family.

Shmuel Leitner spent his teenage years shuttling among seven different concentration camps. At each one, he drew what he witnessed, using scraps of paper such as cement bags as his canvas. Each time he was moved to a new camp, his art was destroyed, and he would re-create it again and again. He survived and later moved to Israel. He rediscovered his brother in Poland after 40 years, each believing the other had perished.

Primo Levi was a Jewish-Italian chemist, partisan, and writer. His account of the year he spent in Auschwitz, *If This is a Man*, was written immediately after the war and published in 1947.

Hanns Loewenbach was born in Germany in 1915. He escaped to Italy and then settled in China with his parents. After the war, he moved to the United States, where he lived until his death in 2012. He is survived by his three children and six grandchildren.

Sister Gertruda Stanislawa Marciniak was a nun of the Elizabethan Order. She ran an orphanage and an adjacent home for girls with tuberculosis. Sister Gertruda used the home as a cover for hiding resistance members and a group of children rescued from a transport set to depart from Warsaw. The children were given forged birth certificates by the local priest, Ludwik Wolski.

Felix Nussbaum was born in Osnabrueck, Germany, and settled in Belgium in 1935. In 1940, Felix was arrested and sent to the Saint Cyprien internment camp in southern France. He escaped and lived in hiding in Brussels until he was caught in 1944 and sent to Auschwitz, where he was murdered.

Dr. Zsuzsanna Abonyi Ozsváth was born in 1931 in Hungary. She survived the war with the help of the family's nanny, Erzsebet Fajo. She is now the director of Holocaust Studies at the University of Texas at Dallas.

Donia Rosen was born in Kosov, Galicia. She was twelve when she hid in the forest after her family was murdered. She survived with the help of Olena Hryhoryszyn, an elderly non-Jewish friend. She immigrated to Israel in 1948.

Yitzkhok Rudashevski was born in 1927 in Vilna, Poland. He and his parents were murdered in the killing pit at Ponary in 1943. His cousin discovered his diary when, after the war, she returned to the hiding place their families had shared.

Sara Selver was born in 1923 in Lodz, Poland. She wrote her diary on the backs of used vouchers in the office of the forced labor camp where she worked. She survived the war and moved to Israel.

Hannah Senesh was a poet whose work has become an integral part of modern Jewish liturgy. She was born in Hungary and moved to Palestine in 1939. In 1944, at the age of twenty-two, she parachuted into Hungary as a member of the Jewish paramilitary Haganah assisting the British army. She was captured and executed.

Zinovii Tolkatchev was a Jew and a member of the Russian armed forces that liberated Majdanek and Auschwitz. Many of his drawings from the liberation of Auschwitz

STORIES (CONTINUED)

were done on the commandant's personal stationery and include the words Kommandantur Konzentrationslager Auschwitz in bold black letters.

Pastor André Trocmé urged his congregation to give shelter to any Jew who should ask for it. With his wife, Magda, he created a haven for persecuted Jews in Le Chabon, France. They were recognized by Yad Vashem as "Righteous Among the Nations" in 1984.

Simcha Unsdorfer was born in 1924 in Czechoslovakia. After his liberation from Buchenwald, he went to England, where he became general secretary of Agudas Israel of Great Britain. His health was severely affected by his years in the camp, and he died in 1968 at age forty-four, survived by a wife and two children.

Rivka Wagner, born in 1924, was the daughter of a rabbi and learned in religious matters. When she was nineteen, she jumped from a moving cattle car to escape certain death in the concentration camps. She survived in Warsaw by pretending to be a non-Jew. She was reunited with her fiancé after the war. They lived in Israel with their four children until her death in 2016.

Dr. Ruth Siegel Westheimer was born in 1928 in Germany. In 1939, at the age of eleven, she was sent to an orphanage in Switzerland, where she survived the war. After the war, she moved to Israel and fought in the War of Independence. She eventually immigrated to the United States and became a well-known expert in sexuality.

Elie Wiesel was awarded the Nobel Peace Prize in 1986 for his activism in the cause of peace, atonement, and human dignity. He was born in 1928 in Hungary and liberated from Buchenwald in 1945. From there he went to France and then to Israel. He lived in the United States until his death in 2016.

Miriam Yahav was born in 1927 in Bialystok, Poland. She moved to Israel in 1949. She died in 2018, having become a great-grandmother.

Jakob Zim was born in 1920 in Sosnowiec, Poland. With his brother Nathan, he was sent on a death march to Buchenwald, where they were liberated. They immigrated to Israel in 1945, where Jacob fought in the War of Independence.

STORIES OF THE PEOPLE PICTURED ON PAGE 20:

Gisi Fleischmann was born in Bratislava, Slovakia (then Pressburg, Austria-Hungary) in 1892. She was a Zionist activist and a leader of the Bratislava Working Group. She was murdered in Auschwitz in 1944.

Izabel and Zoli Marton were twins, born in Dioszeg, Hungary, in 1935 to Lajoz and Ella Marton. They were murdered in Auschwitz.

Yehiel Mintzberg was the son of Abek and Miriam Mintzberg. He was born in Radom, Poland, in 1932. Yehiel was murdered in Treblinka at the age of ten.

Henryk Szwarc was born in Zgierz, Poland in 1893. He was a clothing manufacturer in Lodz, and was married to Mala Eder. He was murdered at Majdanek in 1943.

Shraga Feiwel Picker was born in Sadagora, Romania, in 1857. He lived in Vienna, with his wife **Zipporah**, born in 1860, and their three children. Shraga was a storekeeper, and Zipporah a housewife. They died in Theresienstadt in 1942.

Rudi Salmang was born in Aachen, Germany, in 1898. He was a clerk, married to Mia Frings. He moved to Brussels, Belgium, during the war. He was murdered in Auschwitz.

The **unknown** woman and child are shown in a field outside Lubny, Ukraine, moments before their execution.

Settela Steinbach was born in 1934. She was a Dutch Sinti, sub-tribe of Romani who travelled the Netherlands with their violin orchestras. This photo was taken from a deportation train en route to the work camp Westerbork. Settela was murdered in Auschwitz in 1944.

LOST COMMUNITIES

HERE ARE THE STORIES OF THE COMMUNITIES LISTED ON PAGE 11:

1. **Warsaw, Poland:** The prewar population of Warsaw was 30 percent Jewish. Many Jews died in the ghetto, but the community managed to maintain a semblance of cultural life. When the deportations began, the Jews of Warsaw rose up and fought the Nazis.

2. **Sarajevo, Bosnia, and Herzegovina:** This area was home to both Sephardic and Ashkenazic Jews, a prominent rabbinic dynasty, and a theological seminary. This vibrant community was almost entirely destroyed.

3. **Vienna, Austria:** Jews were prominent in all spheres of life and major contributors to its cultural and scientific achievements. Only a small Jewish community exists today.

4. **Chełm, Poland:** Chełm had a large Jewish community, with a thriving Yiddish and Hebrew culture and a rich religious and political life, and was well-known in Jewish folklore. Today Chełm has no known Jewish residents.

5. **Salonika, Greece:** This two-thousand-year-old Jewish community served as a haven for Jews fleeing Spain during the Inquisition and was the most prolific Sephardic cultural and religious center in the world. This ancient, vibrant culture was completely destroyed.

THE ROMANI

Romani refers to a number of tribes living across Europe. The Romani murdered in the Holocaust were primarily Roma in southeastern Europe and Sinti in Germany, Italy, and France. The history of the Romani in Europe is rife with persecution and discrimination, which continues today in many places.

6 Kielce, Poland: Jews in Kielce were involved in many industries and crafts. Most were murdered in the ghetto or in the camps. A postwar pogrom in 1946 in Kielce convinced many that Europe was still unsafe for Jews.

7 Vilna, Lithuania: Vilna was a major center of Jewish scholarship and culture, with more than fifty thousand Jews. Most of the Jews were murdered in the Ponary forest on the outskirts of town by Nazis and their Lithuanian collaborators. Only a small community remains

8 Frankfurt, Germany: Jews in Frankfurt were prosperous and influential, active in business and politics. Many Jews from Frankfurt fought for Germany in World War I. Of the thirty thousand Jews living in the city before the war, only six hundred survived.

9 Kiev, Ukraine: Kiev was home to a thousand-year-old Jewish community. In 1941, more than one hundred thousand people were murdered at the ravine of Babi Yar near Kiev, including almost thirty-four thousand Jews and many Romani in just two days.

10 Prague, Czech Republic: Prague was home to Jews for more than a thousand years, in a community acclaimed for its literature. Today there is only a small Jewish community.

LEADER'S GUIDE

PLANNING AND PREPARATION

This guided commemoration is flexible and can be held in a variety of settings such as a small group in an intimate setting, a larger group in a social hall or sanctuary, in person or online. It can be led by lay leaders or clergy.

Timing:

The ritual takes about 45 minutes. Using the discussion questions could extend the time to 60-90 minutes.

Materials needed:

- Two candles: use mismatched candlesticks/holders, such as one fancy candlestick and one upside-down tin or glass cup or jar [p3]
- Tea candles candles and matches/lighter [p11]
- Small pieces of paper for each participant, and pen/pencils [p9]
- Fruits with pits: "whole" olives, dates, or cherries, not "pitted" (which have the pits removed). Bite-sized fruits are best. [p17]
- Bread: This should be good bread, to represent the bread of survival and community, not the bread of affliction. [p 25]
- Bread crusts: Any type of bread will do; hard or stale bread is preferable. [p7]
- Wine or juice [p5]

USING THE *MOMENT OF WITNESS* QUESTIONS

Almost every section in this book includes a *Moment of Witness* discussion question. These are designed to give all participants the opportunity to connect their own experiences and the experiences of their community to the issues raised in the text. They are meant as points of connection between participants of all background and life experiences.

When you come to a *Moment of Witness* question, pause and read the question to the group. Allow the group to discuss for a brief period of time, either together or in small groups, before returning to the text.

OPTIONS FOR ADDED RICHNESS

- **Snacks or a meal:** Recipes for dumplings and cookies based on *In Memory's Kitchen*, a cookbook from the Terezin Ghetto, can be found at www.TeachTheShoah.org.
- **Movement:** In Help [p14], have participants walk around the room and find someone they don't know or don't know well, to give them an opportunity to connect with new people.
- **Bread:** On [p25], choose a special bread to honor a particular community. For instance, tsoureki (Greek sweet bread) or babcia bread (Polish sweet bread).
- **Reading:** Reading aloud, whether people take turns, read together, or read responsively, is a powerful way to engage participants with the material. Consider inviting participants to read from the pulpit.
- **Music:**
  - A wordless melody sung or hummed just after lighting the candles in Terror {p10] and the reading of the names of the lost [the pictures in Memory, p20].
  - Songs of strength, e.g. songs written by enslaved people or songs of the underground railroad, will enhance Help, Strength, or Life.
  - Songs of peace work well in Hope.
- **Connection:** In Help [p14], encourage people to reach across the table to someone not sitting next to them.

ALTERNATE EXPERIENCES

- **At home:** This experience works as well in a home setting as in a community context. For the best experience, follow it with dinner and discussion. Meal and recipe suggestions can be found at www.TeachTheShoah.org.
- **For a younger audience:** This commemoration is most appropriate for ages 13+. With a few minor changes, you can make the text age-appropriate for a younger or less knowledgeable group.
  - Terror [p10]: Skip the initial section and go straight to Lost Communities.
  - Awakening [p22]: Cut the first stanza from An Affirmation for the Future.

DISCUSSION QUESTIONS

ALSO SEE THE "MOMENT OF WITNESS" QUESTIONS FOUND THROUGHOUT THE BOOK.

Light and Darkness: Why is it important to talk about how people lived as well as how they died? Survivor Pierre Sauvage said, "If we remember solely the horror of the Holocaust, we will pass on no perspective from which meaningfully to confront and learn from that horror." What do you think he meant by that?

Beginnings: It is natural to believe that shadows are fleeting, that trouble will pass quickly, and that someone else will take care of the world's problems. How can we tell if danger is growing or fading?

Troubles: Notice that we have not mentioned individual perpetrators by name. Atrocities of this magnitude are only possible when many people consent and collaborate. Discuss the many ways people collaborated with the perpetrators (e.g., moving stolen furniture or taking homes after Jews had been forced out; sorting or selling goods sent back from the camps and killing pits; driving trains to the concentration camps). Consider how small acts of willful ignorance and collaboration can slowly build to allow larger atrocities seem normal. How should this inform our response to seemingly isolated acts of bigotry today?

Hiding: Thousands of children were hidden with non-Jewish families, in convents, and in orphanages. Many children in hiding spent the entire war pretending to be someone they were not. How does a child reclaim an identity they have all but lost? Why might they not want to?

Terror: Consider the options Jews had in attempting to escape the Nazis. Where could they go? How could they hide? Jumping from the trains, as Rivka Wagner did [see Stories, p34], was a risky proposition. Most people who jumped were shot by snipers. If they did manage to escape, educated Jews and women had an easier time passing for non-Jews. The risks and difficulty meant saving oneself often involved leaving others behind. Some people gave up the opportunities to escape in order to stay with elderly parents, young children, or other family members. Why would someone make such a choice?

Help: Yad Vashem calls people who helped Jews and other victims of the Holocaust "the Righteous Among the Nations." Many, of course, will never be known, as many were unsuccessful in their attempts to help. Some paid with their lives. Yad Vashem's list of the known Righteous includes more than 25,000 people.

Rescuers often risked not only their own deaths but the deaths of their loved ones. Consider a person's obligations to one's family and to people in need. When is it appropriate to put one's family at risk to help a friend or even a stranger?

Strength: Diaries of victims describe the existence of ghetto libraries, where books circulated in secret among hundreds of people. Discuss the idea of spiritual resistance: resisting the Nazis' attempts at dehumanization by maintaining religious, cultural, and educational practices.

Life: Consider the effect of this experience—the horror, the loss, the fear—on the survivors as they tried to move on with their lives. Many could move on; others, like Eva Heyman's mother, could not [see Stories, p32]. Zsuzsanna Abonyi Ozvath says she judges everyone she meets by whether she believes they would have saved her from the Germans. What do you think it takes to move on from such an experience?

Memory: Elie Wiesel said, "Do we know how to remember the victims, their solitude, their helplessness?" How do we remember the trauma of victims and survivors of traumatic events without traumatizing ourselves?

Awakening: Many of the most famous pictures of the Holocaust were taken by the Nazis with the intent of showing the Jews in an unflattering light. When you think of the pictures and stories from instances of community violence such as the Holocaust, whose perspective are you seeing or hearing? Can you think of stories of those events that are told from the perspective of the victims?

Community: During the Holocaust, the Nazis divided community from community. Discuss the importance of solidarity between communities in nurturing humanity.

Hope: In the section we say, "There is still hope. We can each make a difference."

What kind of difference can an individual make? How can an individual make a difference?

Resolve: Lea Roshkovsky of Yad Vashem used to say that she could end the story of the Holocaust with the yellow star, because the yellow star made everything else inevitable. Once you allow people to be marked as "other," she said, they cease to be human in the eyes of the public and you can do anything you want to them. Discuss how separating people can lead to their dehumanization in the eyes of the rest of society and make bias-motivated violence more likely.

> "During the first days after our return . . . we wanted at last to speak, to be heard . . . . Even so, it was impossible. No sooner would we begin to tell our story than we would be choking over it. And then, even to us, what we had to tell would start to seem unimaginable."
> **(Robert Antelme**, Holocaust survivor, France)

ACKNOWLEDGMENTS

First and foremost, special appreciation goes to our third partner, Michael Fripp, for his insight, ideas, collaboration, and editing. This book would not be what it is without his help.

We would also like to thank Dena Neusner and David Behrman for believing in us and in this most unusual project. A special thank you to Jennifer Zunikoff for adding poetry to our wording. Thank you to our testers: Mehak Burza, Alissa Butler, Jean Fripp, Christine Gallagher, Laura Seiver Gallagher, Jeremy Gordon, Erica Guerra, Tess Haranda, Kim Holden, Julia Joseph, Gay Kelso, John McMath, Vann Millhouse, Dori Morris, Kelton Riley, Anita Sarate, Torrey Schoel, Alisha Tatem, and Bob Troyer. Thank you also to all of our reviewers: Christopher Buckley, Gregory Eftimie, Jean Fripp, Shauntay Larkins, Narayan Srinivasan, and Alisha Tatem.

Thank you to Rabbi Geoffrey Dennis and Congregation Kol Ami, Pastor Whitney Waller-Cole and Creekwood Christian Church, and Pastor Homer Walkup and Lake Shore Baptist Church for helping us pilot this idea.

A most sincere thanks goes to the Yad Vashem International School of Holocaust Studies for teaching us an entirely new way of looking at the Holocaust. Special thanks to Lea Roshkovsky, Adi Rabinowitz-Bedein, Shulamit Imber, Ephraim Kaye, and the teachers at the International School for Holocaust Studies for inspiration and assistance.

ABOUT THE AUTHORS

Deborah Fripp is the president of Teach the Shoah. Deborah has a BS from Stanford University and a PhD from M.I.T. in communication and learning in formal and informal settings. Her website, www.TeachTheShoah.org, provides resources on commemorating, teaching, and understanding the Holocaust for communities, families, and educators.

Violet Neff-Helms, known as Tante to the many religious school kindergarten children she taught for fourteen years, is a freelance writer and the executive vice-president of Teach the Shoah.

Both are alumna of Yad Vashem's How to Teach the Holocaust in Formal and Informal Jewish Education seminar.

SOURCES

2 Hannah Senesh: *Ashrei Hagafrur*, 1944.
4 Miriam Yahav: *My Daughter, Maybe You . . . A Young Girl in Auschwitz* (Beer Sheva, 1994), p. 5.
6 Éva Heyman: *The Diary of Éva Heyman* (Yad Vashem, 1974), p. 80.
7 Yitzkhok Rudashevski: *The Diary of the Vilna Ghetto* (Ghetto Fighters' House, Hakibbutz Hameuchad Publishing House, 1973), p. 19.
8 Ruth Westheimer: *Roller-Coaster Grandma* (Apples & Honey Press, 2018), p. 15.
9 Hannah Gofrit: *I Wanted to Fly Like a Butterfly*, by Naomi Morgenstern (Yad Vashem, 2011), pp. 5, 26.
10 Sara Selver-Urbach: *Through the Window of My Home: Recollections from the Lodz Ghetto* (Yad Vashem, 1971), p. 122.
14 Sister Gertrude Marciniak and Nuro Hoxha: From the collection of Yad Vashem.
14 Zsuzsanna Abonyi Ozsváth: From her talk at "Winning the War: America, Foreign Policy, and the Holocaust," University of Texas at Dallas, June 27, 2018.
15 André Trocmé: From the exhibits at Yad Vashem.
16 Simcha Unsdorfer: *The Yellow Star* (Thomas Yoseloff, 1961), p. 103.
16 Rivka Wagner: Quoted to the authors by her daughter Malky Weisberg.
17 The idea for the fruits with an unbreakable inner core comes from *Haggadah for the Seder for Yom HaShoah veHaGevurah*, ed. Jacobo Rubenstein, 2010.
17 Maya Angelou: Rainbow in the Cloud (Random House, 2014), p. 92.
19 Karaniya Metta Sutta: The Discourse on Loving-Kindness. As translated by Piyadassi Thera, 1999.
20 Donia Rosen: *Forest, My Friend* (Yad Vashem, 1985), p. 94. The original reads, "Not a monument of marble or stone, but one of good deeds, for I believe with full and perfect faith that only such a monument can promise you and your children a better future."
22 Hanns Loewenbach: Quoted in his obituary, "Hanns H. Loewenbach," *Virginian-Pilot*, February 1, 2012. The original quote reads, "Evil does not need your help, just your indifference."
22 Amanda Gorman: The Hill We Climb. From her spoken word poem delivered at the inauguration of President Jospeh R. Biden, 2021.
23 "An Affirmation for the Future": *Days of Remembrance: A Department of Defense Guide for Commemorative Observance* (Office of the Secretary of Defense, 1988), p. 20.
25 Marcia Falk: The Book of Blessings (Beacon Press, Boston, 1996), p.18.
25 Primo Levi: Survival in Auschwitz: If This is a Man, Translated by Stuart Woolf (Orion Press, New York, 2007), p.113.
27 Elie Wiesel: From his Days of Remembrance Address, Washington, DC, 2001.
28 Nelson Mandela: speech at Trafalgar Square, London, February 3, 2005.
29 Bahá'u'lláh: Tablet 6, Words of Paradise, third leaf.
29 Malala Yousafzai: From her speech to the United Nations on her 16th birthday, July 12, 2013.
30 The original quote from Deuteronomy 16:20 reads, "Justice, justice you shall pursue."
40 Pierre Sauvage: *Weapons of the Spirit* (Chambon Foundation, 1989).
41 Robert Antelme: *L'espèce humaine* (Gallimard, 1947), p. 3.
41 Elie Wiesel: From his Nobel Prize Lecture, December 11, 1986. The original reads, "Mankind must remember that peace is not God's gift to his creatures, it is our gift to each other."

CREDITS

Collection of the Yad Vashem Art Museum, Jerusalem, Photos © Yad Vashem Art Museum, Jerusalem: **View of Ostende with Boat,** 1935, by Felix Nussbaum (1904–1944), gouache on paper, 50x64 cm. Gift of Roger-David Katz and his wife Louba Moscicka, Brussels. **Camp Synagogue in Saint-Cyprien,** Brussels, 1941, by Felix Nussbaum (1904–1944), oil on plywood. Gift of Paul and Hilda Freund, Jerusalem. **Rear Entrance, Terezin Ghetto,** 1941-1944, by Bedřich Fritta (Fritz Taussig) (1906-1944), India ink and wash on paper, 51x36.5 cm. Gift of the Prague Committee for Documentation, courtesy of Ze'ev and Alisa Shek, Caesarea. **To the Man who Restored my Belief in Humanity,** 1945, by Yehuda Bacon (b. 1929), gouache, black chalk and pencil on paper, 22.1x30 cm. **Taleskoten,** 1944, gouache, charcoal and crayon on paper, 47.5x58.9 cm, and **Winter**, 1944, charcoal and crayon on paper, both by Zinovii Tolkatchev (1903-1977). Gifts of Sigmund A. Rolat, New York, in memory of his parents, Henryk and Mania, who perished in the Holocaust. **View of Buchenwald, a Few Days after Liberation,** 1945, by Jakob Zim (Cymberknopf) (b. 1920), watercolor on paper, 18.7x29.3 cm. Gift of the artist. **One Spring,** Gurs Camp, 1941, by Karl Robert Bodek (1905-1942) and Kurt Conard Löw (1914-1980), watercolor, India ink and pencil on paper, 14.4x10.3 cm. Gift of Annelies Haymann, Kiryat Bialik. **Liberation** and **Rose and Barbed Wire,** both by Shmuel Leitner. Reprinted with permission of Dr. Gabriel Leitner. Photos on pages 20 courtesy of Yad Vashem Photo Archive Hall of Names.

Shutterstock: background: ilolab; p2, 4, 14, 15: ESB Professional; p9, 27: Picsfive; pIV: Candles: chempina (candlestick), vectortatu (cup), Olli_may (candle), cup: Bodor Tivadar, cherry: Epine, olives: MoreVector, bread, Olga_Zaripova; , paper/pencil: hchjjl; p1: Paul Crash; p6: Valik; p18 (city): vividvic; p31: Masterrr; p36: dikobraziy. Tea candle: Ann D. Koffsky.

Cover art: Shutterstock, Jacob_09

"From Darkness into Light," by Chaim Stern, excerpt from "We pause in reverence" by Alvin Fine from *Gates of Repentance* © 1978, revised 1996 by Central Conference of American Rabbis. Used by permission of CCAR. All rights reserved. "From Tomorrow On," by Motele: *Through Our Eyes: Children Witness the Holocaust,* by Itzhak Tatelbaum, Yad Vashem, 2004, p. 89. Reprinted with permission. "They are gone," by Jennifer Zunikoff: excerpt modified from her poem "Leo Is Gone," written in loving memory of Leo Bretholz, March 9, 2014. "A Day Will Come," by Jennifer Zunikoff, 2018, Reprinted with permission. "Still Stands," by Karen Webber, 2023. Reprinted with permission.

STILL STANDS

At the base of the Tree of Life,
potatoes grow,
dug up each spring,
proclaiming,
"Let all who are hungry come and eat."

A forceful gale blasts gold coils
like branches
twisting, swirling, falling to a heap.

But, new spirals spring,
face the sun,
as the tree sucks the
sweet wine up from ancient wells.

Day will come
When oranges bitter sweet
with sprigs of rosemary will dance.
When branches will hold names
for peace, salaam, samaya, shalom.
When a reprise of a sacred song dangles,
spinning out an entire world.
When fruits and leaves and turns of phrase fall silent
One word will sing—
Halleluyah.

(Cantor Karen Webber)